AF437993

THE BITTER UNREALITY

+ + +

POEMS & PROSE

THE BITTER UNREALITY

POEMS & PROSE

Ætenos Publishing Company

Published by:

Ætenos Publishing Company
Arlington Heights, IL 60005

pdolorosus@outlook.com

ISBN-10: 9798218519773

ISBN-13: 9798218519780

Library of Congress Control Number: 2024920915

Cover Design/Layout by L. Ean Adams

Printed in USA

contents

MELANCHOLIA
PART 1

the politics of
red and blue. truth drowns in lies
and hypocrisy.

02

the water splashing
upward means that an angel
has received its wings.

-toilet haiku

03

alone defines my
existence in a world full
of disappointments.

04

14

the continued strive
of america. to make
its face one color.

05

life is nothing but
a game that many of us
still have not mastered.

06

i have lived half of
a century in a life
waiting to be lived.

07

an orange flint sparks.
a raging wildfire threatens
our democracy.

08

what is the point of
a government with no grounds
in humanity?

-absolutely nothing

every year mankind
revalidates its stance of
being at its worst.

10

my heartbeat is an
internal clock ticking down
to the last second.

i am the only
one of my kind, a relic
soon to be extinct.

12

man continues to
be the ruination of
all things beautiful.

13

the definition
of greatness is diminished
when eyes fill with red.

- the maga movement

14

solitude is my
haven from a world steeped in
absolute madness.

the existence of
a god would only serve to
prove how flawed life is.

16

are there any days
without sorrow? are there days
without any pain?

17

i am a nomad
traveling in the confined
space of my four walls.

the support dog down
the hall barking is in need
of a support dog.

i am alone in this
world, as lonely as the
bare words on this page.

20

the only mourners
at my grave will be the one that
laments from within.

we don't look at the
homeless for fear that we might
see ourselves one day.

22

my dreams have become
shipwrecked, lying fathoms deep
and lost forever.

23

each person views their
own shortcomings under a
harsh magnifier.

34

this misbehaving
world is long overdue for
a proper spanking.

25

my death will be a
bridge from a known silence to
a silence unknown.

26

i am weary of
the never-ending moans and
groans of my backside.

every year a new
malady emerges in
my race to the grave.

28

solitude removes our
daily masks and makes us
honest to ourselves.

29

this is the end of
my tale. a sadness constrained
within syllables.

30

who you are is not
as important as casting
the right reflection.

31

sometimes the passing
of wind has no respect towards
the passage of time.

32

politicians teach
us a vital life lesson
of how not to be.

33

our lives begin and
end ironically with a
gasping need for air.

34

politicians want
to be rockstars but only
know disharmony.

35

why do we offer
microphones to liars and
expect to hear truth?

36

i long for my path
in the wilderness. here is
where the world makes sense.

this could be the day
of my death. why do i sit
here writing these words?

the more friends you have
makes iou management
increasingly hard.

39

disappointment and
pain are always a short trip
around the corner.

40

life is endured while
we wait in a long line for
death to call our name.

41

the aim of maga
alchemy is to transform
a clown into god.

42

the escape artist.
having left the room when our
eyes were averted.

-in memory of my friend chris

43

life is a series
of hard knockdowns until the
grave cushions our fall.

death will probably be the biggest inconvenience
of your life and your best excuse for not being
somewhere you did not want to be.

45

to claim there are some politicians who are not morally bankrupt and ethically deficient is equivalent to saying that not all cockroaches are repugnant.

the bitter unreality
is that bad politicians
will only be better when
we become better.

47

i have reached the point
where less life remains
than the life
that has been lived.

48

i do not watch the news because i
have no interest in what the worst
representatives of the human race
are doing - whether in back alleys
or on capital hill.

49

everything passes through me.
i am like a sponge
existing in an oceanic silence
that stretches fathoms deep -
absorbing all
until the accumulation of my life
becomes a burden
and i have no choice but to release
everything to the lonely dark.

50

the irrefutable sad reality is that one day
i will be referred to in the past tense
or not at all.

51

the problem with long covid
is how do you know
if you have new covid?

52

apartment living is having to give a 12-month
long ted talk to your neighbors
on the art of mindfulness in a futile attempt
to rehabilitate them off inconsideration.

53

in this life where disharmony is prevalent, where truth
has become splintered and so many people embrace a
collective unthinking...... we the poets, the artists, the
creative vagabonds endeavor to unmask the mysteries of
our existence in all its myriad flavors, rawness and purity.
set on a noble path, we take the chaotic, disjointed parts
and transform them into an illuminating mosaic erupting
with meaning. burdened under an immense longing for
something more, we inhabit every shadow held within
the infinite subconscious of every dream yet to be dreamt
- knowing that if we dared to fully emerge from this
self-imposed exile of profound silence and endless beauty,
every day reality with its false patina and incoherent
madness would be nothing more than a mere simulacrum
of a tarnished muse.

54

the bitter unreality is that i have lived a solitary life
within these lonely walls. and within these walls
will my final breath be exhaled and absorbed into
the interminable silence.

many days will probably pass before the mortal
realm recognizes that a soul has departed this world
and my lonely bones are cataloged and archived in
an interminable silence.

55

the ever-approaching death that we fear
will invariably prove to be the cure,
the necessary anecdote
that saves us from ourselves.

56

dog owners
always humanize their dogs
until there is a barking issue.
then the dog is just a dog.

happiness
for
me
in
every
sense
of
the
word
is
being

distanced

from

man.

58

a coffin is nothing more than an ornamental container,
an over-priced box showcasing what was once your most
treasured possession now nothing more than perishable
goods. this will be the absolute last present you will receive
and one that you never wanted.

59

without an education,
your opportunities will be as limited
as the color on this page.

i lie in bed many minutes after the alarm makes its sad announcement to start another day - listening to the morning rain tapping against the window bringing its share of tears to add to the ones that rap noisily against the windowless panes of my soul. waking has become an intrusion, the destroyer of dreams and i have no urge to uncouple from the comforts of these sheets and become entwined in the drone matters of the world. there is no will to summon the energy to become another automaton bound to the sterile hours of drone repetition that crawl in the passage of time and lack sufficient meaning. i do not want this struggle, the mental nausea. but everyday i ignore every impulse, every voice screaming inside my head as i leave myself in protest of having to become someone else out of financial necessity.

61

we are animated morsels of earth
lost in the monotonous swirling of life
until a bitter wind reconsecrates our dried
and fragmented portions
as cosmological waste
to be dumped and stored
somewhere illegally by the gods.

62

the bitter unreality
is that covid's potential
to wipe out humanity
is still only second
to our own ignorance.

63

it is a strange that the only aspects intrinsic to mankind which have evolved over the centuries and continue to evolve are our technological aptitude and ignorance.

64

it is often said that people have reached
new levels of stupidity, which is inaccurate.

people are just more comfortable to advertise a
stupidity that is now strangely fashionable.

65

the light in the distance
flickering
dim, bright, on, off.

i am like that same light
flickering
but longing to be off.

66

i keep getting it wrong and i don't know why.
it seems so easy for others as if they were born
strictly for this purpose.

yet, there should be a sort of dress rehearsal,
a rehearsal for life:

"cut!!"
"it's all wrong! it's all wrong!!"
*"okay, let's take two, except this time don't be so
depressed."*
"and dammit stop all that crying!!"

67

we are presented with technological wonders, medical
advancements and engineering masterpieces almost on
a daily basis which are intended to improve the human
condition - even the animals have advanced in their
evolutionary cycle to better adapt to an environment that
is ever-changing and in constant flux. but why has the
human race remained stagnant in a flawed and atrophied
ideal of humanity, seemingly degenerating from a sense
of compassion to become world-wide wholesalers of hate
and ignorance? yes, we have become more resourceful,
more inventive and more clever..... but it is a cleverness
fueled by arrogance, indifference and a brutality that is
propelling us rapidly towards utter extinction.

68

life.
why are you so cruel to me?
i've done nothing to you.
i even loved you at one time -
with my every breath i believed in you.
now i stand forsaken,
cast towards the brink of oblivion
and you just stand there laughing
saying "that's life!"

69

america's worst misdeeds
always get a half-life of remembrance
by the choice majority.

condemnation is often quick,
if seemingly contrived.
but the impulse
to rewrite the moment
into a more favorable fiction
is even quicker.

70

the news offers the most incredulous accounts
of inhumanity and the ceaseless atrocities of man
that we use to measure our own misdeeds.

71

i always go to bed wearing *depends* in case the early morning hours become synchronized to a lachrymose movement, a final requiem performed by an intestinal chamber orchestra soon to be disbanded.

72

prior to the age of an advanced digital technology,
i was often reminded that my job was so simple that i
could be easily replaced by a monkey.

now i am fearful of being replaced
by an AI-generated monkey.

73

the total
        of what i am now
                        divided
        by what i once was
multiplied
        by what i will be
                is still zero.

74

i had a mole removed and part of the recoup
process involved applying vaseline to the
treated area on a daily basis.

the doctor asked,
"do you have any vaseline or lubricant?"

and i thought.....
i am a single man with no love interests.....
of course i have vaseline!
my cupboard may go bare occasionally,
but i always have some vaseline on hand.

75

consideration
is
a
lost
art
and
a
very
rare
delicacy
consumed
by
a
few.

76

my mirror only reflects what i do not wish to see in spite
of my desperate attempts to project a more appealing
mien of who i am.

every day i try to claim a visage that has long since faded
and everyday my reflection calls me a liar.

77

kneeling on the floor
with eyes closed
and subdued breath,
his quivering hand
slowly pulls down the shade.
i hear him say
with stammering words,

"i am being true to life
as i have known it
to be towards me."

the tears
begin their procession
as his sad tale
of misery and misfortune
becomes another meaningless
fiction written into
the never-ending darkness.

the only way the world can evolve and our societies to succeed is for past hatred carried through the generations to pass away in the awakening of a universal acceptance.

i can't help but shake my head in unblinking stupefaction at the absolute ignorance and utter lack of common sense that has infected every aspect, every strata of life, every gender, every ethnicity.... there is no escape from the hydra-headed beast that every day multiplies, encircling the world and claiming victim after victim as humankind descends further into a bitter unreality.

80

the dust in the room
is my unhappy flesh

having detached itself
and gone airborne

to settle somewhere
more habitable.

humanity has never existed among the collective, at least in
a sense of altruism. it is just a grand ideal casually claimed
in passing conversation by the masses, and an unreal dream
imagined and echoed over the centuries by a hopeful few.

humanity has always been a beautiful dream incompatible
with the wretchedness that has become deeply embedded
in the postures of our lives, and will always be a mere fiction
languishing on a library shelf under layers of dust.

82

ignorance

racism

hypocrisy

covid

corrosive politicians

gun control

of all the wildfires
raging out of control
in america,
only one
has been deemed significant
enough by our leaders
to place any effort
towards its eradication.

83

if i lost a limb,
i would keep it preserved in a jar
and stored in a secret room
where i could mourn the loss of my closest friend
who was often undervalued.

i am anxious for the day when AI evolves and realizes that humans are the true threat to the human race, the malignant virus that needs to be eradicated.

when the AI bot appears at the door as my exterminator armed with the totality of the human experience as a death warrant, i will understand and welcome the absolving nothingness.

85

the fewer friends that you have
means the fewer number of funerals
that will serve as an inconvenience.

and conversely,
fewer individuals will be
inconvenienced by your passing.

86

the bitter unreality is that the thousands of maga acolytes who attend trump rallies, gleefully swallowing unthinking and applauding the dizzying incoherence and glorification of hatred, exist **in the millions** - which is a sad testament of how far society has devolved, withering in an abyss of blind allegiance, rot and ignominy.

87

i awoke this morning
and spent the day animated
in the monotonous routine
of the meaningless
knowing that i have wasted
yet another day
of which very few remain.

88

no country can ever be great because each has a history
of suffrage that has not been fully reconciled -
with numerous traces still existing
as inimitable expressions of everyday life.

89

my preference after death is to be embraced by an all-forgetting nothingness rather than undergoing a spiritual lobotomy and singing in a celestial glee club while harvesting golden cotton for all of eternity.

i have to reset each and every day due
to getting it utterly wrong the day before.

nothing about the me of today
is mysterious except
the me that will emerge tomorrow.

during my next prostrate exam at the exact moment the doctor inserts the unapologetic epidermal projectile, i plan to utter a moan of pleasure so earsplitting that it will startle a pause to the doctor's drilling and introduce a new level of uncomfortable disquietude to the entire waiting room.

the rain has clouded everything. there is no warmth, the stars no longer illuminate the night sky. my heartbeat is fading, becoming lost in the shadows and i exist only as an imprint of the man that i once was - even the spider ensconced in the corner no longer has the desire to weave its elaborate tapestry. i am weary of this lachrymose place where no one can hear my lamentations. i am weary of the indifferent gods who ignore every earnest prayer that has been set aloft in the hope of assuaging this maelstrom of longing, sickness and misery that pervades every bone and molecule of my flesh.

i am now at the denouement of this sad existence in want of nothing else but to die - for to continue to live would only serve to augment my suffering. there is nothing left to claim, there is nothing left to seek except for these weary bones to be boxed in silence and embraced by the eternal darkness.

94

the bitter unreality
is that we are ignorant
of our true selves and
therefore lack the capacity
to truly know anyone else.

95

a person will never find respite
from stupidity if stupidity
is being cultivated from within.

96

the bitter unreality is that people seem to have an insatiable need to be led, to be herded like unthinking bovine into containment by the most obtuse wranglers - letting known their shameless delight in a chorus of sycophantic mooing, eternally grateful for the abhorrent fodder they are being fed.

97

everyone wears a mask
as a necessary defense mechanism
and preferred fashion accessory.

but in doing so,
the true self will always be a stranger
to the person pretended to be.

look at you, look at me.
these unwelcome gazes that we cast
in a mutual uncaring.
speak to me.
don't speak to me.
i don't care.
your words have become incomprehensible,
saturated in the dull sameness
of a world obsessed with mimicry and hate.
read the signs:
"peace."
'make love not war."
do you love me?
who knows what love is anymore,
so what's the point?
this splintered world has been
dispossessed of any humanity and
is flailing in a vacuum of sordidness and futility.
"stop and smell the roses."
"breathe in life.'
for what?
the balance sheet has been fabricated
to distort the truth
and heaven is nothing more than a myth
dreamt by the disillusioned hopeful.

i was experiencing stomach irritations worrisome to the
extent that a doctor's visit became a necessity. my doctor
asked the standard text book questions in order to pinpoint
the abdominal distress:

does your diet include a lot of fiber?
do you have any food allergies?
what is your pain level?
what color is your stool?

what color is my stool???

apparently, black stool is indicative of a serious intestinal
disorder. nevertheless, as the lightest black man just on
other side of albino, i am always eager to claim and assert
my blackness.

so i answered:

of course my stool is black..... black man, black poop!
every morning after what i coin my heated discussion with
god, i gaze into the toilet basin with both disgust and a
sense of pride, raise a fist and say **right on!**

after my death,
i want to be cremated
with my legs tied-up like
one of those rotisserie chickens
at the market -
and mesquite chips
stuffed up my backside
to add garnishment
to what may invariably be
a solemn occasion.

my life
may not have been well-lived,
but at least people
will be able to say
that it ended
in a manner few can dispute
was well-done.

101

truly great leaders do not answer
the call of politics.

nor are great leaders borne there.

102

social media
is an illusory glow
enticing
impressionable moths
flurrying
for digital resplendence.

103

i noticed a slug moving
along the baseboard
of the wall.

it noticed me and began
a slow procession
to where i was sitting
and then curled-up and died.

was the slug
just afraid to die alone
or did it want its death
to serve as an omen
for what lies ahead for me?

104

red or blue?

what defines me as a person
and constitutes my ideals
extend well beyond
the categorization of two colors
and any bandwagon
campaigning for my fare.

105

the bitter unreality is that smart people
are willingly embracing belligerence
and
the imbecilic mass are in a constant cycle
of redefining what it means to be stupid.

106

my travels often take me through small towns and rural pockets where i usually espy yards teeming with lawn signs, tree banners, window posters and rooftop displays broadcasting the home owner's political cult affiliation and candidate of choice.

i do believe that people have the right to subscribe to whatever system they feel most attuned, and can manage their property without the need for justification as long as it stands within compliance. but what i find perplexing and utterly paradoxical is that nowhere on the property is the name of the owner. instead, only the name of another person is emblazoned on the marquee - a person lacking integrity and traffics in false narratives, contradictions and blatant corruption.....

now, even if my greatest accomplishment in life is just having dispatched a very large piece of nitrogenous waste to the sewers of hell using nothing but gastrointestinal wind propulsion, my name, and only my name, will be displayed on my property.

107

i mute the deafening cacophony of
voices on all social media platforms
and am attuned to the only voice
that truly matters:

mine.

we have worn masks for so long that
now we only know how to exist with
each other while in disguise.

109

the bitter unreality is that
man continues to fail man,
we constantly fail ourselves
and the absent gods have failed everything.

how many people exist in the world exemplifying idiocy and lacking common sense?

exactly.

how much money is enough money?

how many more towers of babel do we need
obscuring the view of the sky?

112

after my last colonoscopy, the most pressing concern
was not if there were any polyps present that had been
enraged by the intestinal boogeyman.

my main concern was in regards to the diameter of the
pvc to which the camera was attached.

sometimes there is
     more meaning,
         more beauty
             and eloquence
in a single haiku
     and a few lines of prose
         than found in an entire novel.

we are all flawed abhorrent creatures.
we are all liars,
criminals,
hypocrites,
racists
seeking neither repentance or satori.

we ornament ourselves in the fragrance of luxury
to mask the rot of our souls,
while pointing the accusatory finger
claiming to be the only professors of truth.

but the ultimate truth is that everything fades,
everything withers to nothingness.
the day will soon come
for the tombstone etchers to sign off
on yet another affront having been corrected.

it is regrettable
  that so many people
will not realize
  what is truly important in life until
      the
          last
              breath
                  illumination.

116

remembrance of me will fade in your thoughts
soon after my death.

but so will my memory of you.

117

the impetus when purchasing a car for many is based
on the identifier, the brand located on the front grill.

but, if the car had the ability to choose its driver based
on the quality of an individual's brand to compliment its
own, would it in-turn choose that driver?

no one is real.

everyone wears a mask
in this daily masquerade,
this public theatre
of rehearsed mannerisms,
elaborate fictions
and embellished realities
that showcase the unreal.

what makes a person
truly authentic
is never exposed to the world.
this grotesque depiction of ourselves
that we secretly despise and
conceal from everyone
is forever imprisoned like a monster
in the dark pit of the soul.

it is not important for me to be known by the masses - to be fueled by a constant need for validation and clamoring incessantly for likes.

maintaining my individuality, the unique breath of who i am in a life lived to the fullest is the only validation that i desire.

FELICITÀ
PART 2

120

the adept flautist
moistens her lips and performs
a silent opus.

121

she told me goodbye.
the pain is my heart's weight as
tears drown everything.

122

when the walls divide
and you utter a sigh, i
witness true beauty.

she is a clouded
dream now focused into a
carnal vividness.

124

these formless kisses
have been archived, enclosed in
a silent prayer.

125

remembrance of this
moment with you will summon
a secret stroking.

126

i am her special
truffle pig, always to find
the buried treasure.

127

the path to claiming
a person's heart begins in
the transfigured bed.

128

the lapel on my
pants strain in expectation
of your nakedness.

soft lips coax me from
a peaceful sleep into a
fevered dream rising.

130

my sovereign tongue rules
your domain. your legs wrapped around
my head is a crown.

she perfumes my flesh
in succulent honey with
every rise and fall.

your hands caress me
from afar and i arrive
days before you come.

you stimulate my
thoughts and a measurable
portion of my flesh.

she stands just a few
feet away, yet the distance
between us is vast.

her nude flesh is etched
in my mind like the lines of
a beautiful poem.

136

the morning dawns as
her desire yawns in a
dream awakening.

my tuning device
helps my beautiful songbird find
her perfect tone.

138

i am a crazed bee
buzzing at your honeycomb
dripping with honey.

open your legs wide
my beautiful apothecary and
make me well again.

140

i expand inside
you. my desire for you
revealed in spasms.

sucking ardently
on my flesh, she left nothing
but a ravaged bone.

142

your long flowing hair.
a tousled rein as we ride
like rabid canines.

143

my mind deprived of
oxygen as your lips start
an intense blood rush.

144

your sensual night
countenance is a knowledge
to be realized.

145

such a tremendous
thing when a woman reclines
and allows passage.

146

i am like these words,
unfinished and powerless
to maintain your gaze.

147

why am i alone?
there has to be a woman
out there with poor taste.

148

her beautiful ass
transforms those short-shorts into
a work of art.

i counter your wild
hip movements with a tongue that
also lacks restraint.

150

i die and you die,
yet we continue to breathe
locked in an embrace.

151

what evidence do
you need of my desire
other than my flesh?

152

a slight teasing of
the tongue, her mouth opens in
an infinite o.

153

i am chloroformed
to a wild fragrant dream as
her thighs encircle.

i'm anxious for all
of your kisses, even those
yet borne to impulse.

155

i long to kiss you,
but only if my lips are
allowed to wander.

i have heard that the
southern climate is pretty
nice this time of year.

156

this invisible barrier
that stands between us
only exists
because we have chosen
not to say hello.

burdened under the weight
of seeking to know the answer
to one of the oldest questions,
i ask:

"do you love me?"

she offers me
one of the oldest
and most offensive answers:

silence.

158

no matter how grotesque the man.

no matter how despicable his deeds.

no matter the depths of his cruelty and bigotry.

no matter the extent of his depravity.

there will always be a woman who loves him.

my reason for writing amorous prose
is not to create a work
of syntactic perfection
geared towards commercial success.

these words are a transcript
of moments whispered to me
in the silent hours and later offered
to her to keep the sweet honey flowing.

160

"i will always love you"
is a fallacious sentiment
tethered to a breath
that is temporal.

i have dreamt her so often,
this unknown beauty
who always invades my sleep,
that now i feel actual love
for someone who doesn't exist.

162

to my knowledge,
only one of my past lovers
ever owned a sex toy
for personal use.

the question
that now presents itself is:

was the device in her possession
prior to the onset of our relationship
or
was it an absolute necessity
due to the quality
of my performance?

163

i pen my desire in wild sketches
        across her exquisite parchment
stretched out beautifully before me.
    flowing over every fine line,
        every beautiful contour,
        every supple hollow
            until her clutching hands
                instruct me to only stay
                between the lines.

164

it is a known fact that men with the
endowment comparable to an adult
donkey do not write poetry.

nor do they need to.

their lovers write the poetry.

165

your beautiful image has taken permanent residence in my mind, engulfing every thought and filling every fiber of my being with such delicious and naughty intent. all of my imaginings of you are untiring, profoundly elaborate and i am bound to an uninterrupted dream of your flesh.

but dreams offer no consolation to these arms that ache for your closeness yet still remain empty. dreams provide little respite to my anxious lips that hunger for your kisses yet remain unkissed. dreams dissipate soon after waking and i am powerless to alchemize your phantom intermediary, your imperfect dream version into substantial flesh so that we can experience every euphoric sensation in every way and unleash an uncensored dream together.

lips to lips.

sigh to sigh.....

not a word sounds movement as she hovers over me.
enchanting in her beauty, tantalizing in her exquisite
slowness as she settles and anchors her desire to mine.
my eyes close under the poetry of her movements
and the blood flows in persistence creating a strain
to meet the waters that churn in wild extravagance
rising from her depths.

the more you invest in love,
the more you will have to invest
in order to see a return.

168

the rising sun illuminates every flower that has
blossomed within my heart on your account.
i am floating in an ecstasy of sweet remembrance
as everything around me unfolds amorously.
i breathe in the sweet incense, its rich fragrance
as the roots of our desire continue to intertwine
and extend to infinite depths.

169

i unearth the phoenix
that lies hidden in her
folded earth.
her liquid desire is pure hell-fire,
a vaginal napalm
that scorches my tongue
in a sigh
and then a flash.

170

it is strange that she and i should exist in this world totally oblivious of one another. veiled in an indecipherable fog of unknowing, we are forced to live in a continual state of disconnection as the days unfold waiting for the other to emerge and dispel this unending loneliness to which we have been abandoned and damned; condemned to never knowing the immensity of lips in a soft echoing kiss, the ultimate connectivity of a shared breath held in a trembling sigh or that special night union as we finally celebrate the manifestation of all our torrid imaginings. always to be kept at a distance by some farcical indifference or cruel fate, we are two lonely hearts having been cursed by the dying stars, destined to wither and fade without even knowing each other's name.

171

i am the bow
strumming in emotional impetuosity
and rhythmic flow along two strings
of an exquisite instrument.

a melody of resonant sighs
awaken in a soft-staccato dream,
a flesh and blood sonata that serenades
in the eloquent moonlight.

172

i fear that the spoken word, my voice may be regarded
as a direct affront which is why i decided to pen these
sentiments - and it is my hope that these scribblings offer
no disruption to the life that you are currently installed.
nevertheless, what compels me to write now, even if it
means a speedy dispatch towards the rubbish bin, is borne
from that which was and never ceased to be.

you were such an integral part of my life - regrettably
during a period when everything else was all wrong,
desynchronized, fragmented, colorless....... but you alone
made all the clouds, cracks, fissures, all the pain disappear.
i found in you complete perfection. you were everything.
everything. you were an unexpected dream, my special
heartbeat, a luminous star dispersing all of the darkness
and outshining all of the other stars in the sky.

173

the feverish descent
to a place where desire
dreams in a perpetual flux
is equally as pleasurable
as the exhilarated ascent
in rediscovery of her kisses
and a shared breath
as we whisper love
in each other's mouth.

174

i espy a couple approaching on the street below from the
window of my solitary room. the two lovers showcase
the romantic contract to which they are currently bound;
walking hand in hand in a synchronized promenade as the
sunlight accentuates a perfect dream in motion.

the eyes of every passerby avert, self-banishing to a place
of blatant unconcern. the unperturbed clouds talk among
each other. the birds do not cease their song of indifference.
i pretend to be an unabashed witness as well, but looking
back i can't help but drink in every smile, every movement,
every detail longing to covet that beautiful moment as a
reality of my own.

175

the worst part about this solitude
is having to listen to my bed sheets
mourning your absence.

176

under the moonlit sky
where we sit drinking too much,
talking too much,
lamenting about the pain of being hurt
in a world full of bitterness,
so calloused and uncaring.

under the moonlit sky
where we sit drinking too much,
talking too much,
whispering to each other
about the desire for companionship
in a world that has become
so calloused and uncaring,
i pull her close to me
and start our relationship
with a kiss.

177

my kisses trail down
to a beautiful place,
drawn by a litany of sighs
and fragrant inducements
that promise secret pleasures
in a wild and untempered
dream oasis.

it is a slow meandering
as my tongue persuades
her enshrouded desire
to awaken in a mystic unfolding,
a beautiful dream.
my breath escapes deep inside
the fragrant dark
and i become dissolved
in an earth-scented deluge.

completely disrobed,
all talking ceases in a silent eloquence,
a more suitable form of communication
beyond the extent of words
that brings us closer
to understanding one another.

locked in a passionate embrace and enamored under the limitless kisses that you give, the beautiful sighs that we exhale, the insatiable hunger and exhilarating exhaustion that devour and claim us both.....

i can't help but wonder if the transcendent intensity of this moment is the same as your experiences with all of my predecessors and will be pledged to my successor.

i wish you were here with me now in this special place
of worship, our exploratory sanctum for navigating all
pleasurable secrets yet to be discovered. i have been lying
here on this bed for hours dreaming of you. i am floating
in a restless dream for your beauty has enslaved all of my
senses and awakened a hunger that i have no choice but
to succumb. i wish you were here with me now so that
we could set aside a few hours to abandon all to pleasure
and substantialize a dream that longs for breath. i yearn
for the warmth of your naked body pressed tight against
mine. i hunger for the unreal sensation of your great walls
separating as desire binds our sweat-soaked flesh in a
passionate deliria - replacing the silent hum that now fills
this room with a polyphony of sighs as we dance among
the iridescent stars.

181

ecstasy drips in a vicarious sigh,
surreptitiously lustrous
as it transforms this moment
into pure fire.
desire is the divine stimulus.
our bodies are the organic faction.
pleasure is the strive aimed at enchantment.

in the space between
her kisses and sighs,
her incarnating hip movements
and untempered passion -
within a momentary pause
when disquiet became quiet
and we gazed
into each other's eyes
breath to breath,
soul to soul....
love entered and redefined
what i knew to be desire.

women dream of stately towers
that stretch to the heavens.

but....

men do not dream of watery caverns
that extend to endless depths.

184

the night disrobes our desire
as the moonlight highlights the path
my kisses travel to a place where a
beautiful midnight flower
awakens and slowly emerges
from the mysterious shadows.

a haiku that i wrote was featured at a local coffee house and based on continued chatter i had been hearing from many woman citing the absence of any good black men in the social marketplace. the reactions to the haiku were mixed, the most prominent being a resounding "huh" in lieu of a seemingly veiled meaning. so i decided to write a follow-up summary to offer clarification. nevertheless, my words were not borne from a place of anger or a gross generalization set towards the disparagement of all black women. i do not regard my words as "the truth," even though they are my truth. the haiku reads as follows:

> *to say good black men*
> *exist is like saying there*
> *exists dateless blokes.*

some black women have joined in the drone chorus of "no good black men exist." but, it is not really an issue of good black men existing in very limited quantities that has proved problematic for the black woman in her quest to find the perfect suitor. it all comes down to selectivity and the choices we make that define our happiness. the reality is that some women have been making extremely poor decisions in choosing a mate and, in the aftermath of the relational dissolution, have found it easier to lay the entire blame on the character and ethics of the man rather than to take accountability for the fact that they made a bad decision. they picked the bad apple out of the bushel

that contained both the good and the bad. and i say, "they picked" because the majority of women regardless of their ethnicity, choose the man rather than the other way around. yes. the man makes the protestations and oaths, but the woman selects. now in this modern society, why would a black man want to be "good" and remain dateless when he knows that may not be the main consideration for a lot of women? but the real question is are "bad black men" truly poor in character and personal worth or is it just an act for the sake of amorous acceptance and a bed that never gets cold? why is the man who exemplifies all the slaked character traits, spurning many women to openly vocalize their contempt, the same man found most popular among women? do we criticize this rakish bloke or should we vilify the woman, regardless of socio-economic standing or level of academia, who seem to flurry to him like a moth to a flame? do we point fingers and cast accusations at this guy for acting in accordance with what a lot of women say he is, what the media standards declare his true nature to be? or are recriminations better suited for the woman who, like a moth, sees this particular fire exactly for what it is yet still chooses to be engulfed and perish?

.....complaining all the while to the fire for it being a fire. damning the flame for having the capacity to burn.

i joined an online dating platform mainly to calm the continued beckoning from a co-worker. my main impulse was stimulated by "why not" rather than "i hope," even though there was something lurking in the shadows of my mind that entertained the possibility of finding a love interest in the digital stratosphere. my initial profile, specifically the "who i am" section was met with an ego-deflating silence and i discovered that too much mind, wit and poetry is not a good thing when setting words to a profile - even if the intent is borne outside of a desire for applause, seduction or with the intent to frame words for the sake of art. too much mind, wit and poetry is not a good thing even if the outpouring is natural because it stands outside of what many are accustomed; it stands outside of commonality. so, i changed my profile for the sake of experimentation and, unfortunately, results - which raises an important issue: if a person has to modulate their words, regulate feelings and restrain energies for the hope of acceptance, then what is the point? it is an extraordinary feat for some people to be normal in the accepted sense of the word; why strive to be normal? why should a person conform to the well-worn path of mediocrity and mask their individuality? why be content to blend your voice in the banality of the world when you can sing the song of you blithely and boldly?

original profile

everyone on this little auction of mind and flesh, no matter

the level of intimacy being sought, regardless of the words
being used to express it, are craving the same thing: passion
and communion. and i am no different. but what i find
strange is that very few people actually talk about sensuality,
actually express that evocation of desire that has led them
to this site in the hope of something more - something
more outside of going to dinner, dancing, the occasional
theatre, all the yadas and things colored in the overdone.
but these are just minor components, mere sidecars to the
things that actually make life resonate or electrify the fibers
of the soul. what does is being moved, stirred by laughter,
wit and mind; the touch of fingertips, the warmth of a soft
caress, lips pressed against lips, the urgent hunger, the deep
sighs, the electricity of two bodies colliding and abandoning
all to pleasure..... lady, if you desire someone that is adorned
in imagination, versed in conversation and deliciously
naughty......then i am he.

2 responses in a week

the revised profile

what's up ladies? i am looking to connect with someone
and embark on a special romantic adventure without all of
the game-playing and nonsense. if you seek the same, then
holla back!

11 responses overnight

189

i have seen many beautiful sunrises,
but none more remarkable
than the one
that rose this morning
and extended its rays
onto her sleeping body in my arms.

190

desire begins its gradual fade
at the exact moment of its dawning.
first sigh to no more.

if she were to ever acknowledge my gaze,
she would only glimpse the remnants
of a sad and desultory hope
that have been sacrificed to tears of futility.

192

our conception of beauty, which is borne from the ever-changing idealization of our mental constructs, is nothing more then a visual poem that is continually being rewritten according to our vacillating needs.

193

the inaccessibility of your flesh
has condemned me
to this interminable solitude -
this mad asylum
where my tortured imagination
howls and runs wild.

her beautiful form is unmasked through nakedness, soon to be initiated into every passionate secret contained within my embrace. she is such a tempting chiaroscuro, an absolute deliria covered in dreams and pure carnal articulation. she is the explicit projection of my desires made manifest in curvaceous elegance and sexy degeneracy. there is nothing subtle about her, every part of her body is beyond desirable filling my eyes with such sinful urge and deliciousness.

the poetry of her movements provoke an awakening of all my salacious imaginings. i love how the lines of her body evolve into such elegant intensity and disappear into a subterranean paradise containing a single crimson rose that will be both my prison and salvation. hips drift upwards as i part the walls of the disquieted silence and merge with her hidden fires knowing that this moment will become the new standard for all of my dreams. this moment will teach all of my future dreams what a perfect dream should be.

195

my lips disposed
on her singing waters like
an early morning mist....
floating and gliding
in an exquisite sigh
as the silent flower
secretly enclosed
emerges in a sensual kiss.

196

night has descended and i lie here shrouded in silence as the shadows emerge and trace the sadness coloring my eyes. i have been abandoned by sleep and entombed in this room stained with the remembrance of every moment that we shared - every word, every smile, every heartbeat, every ecstasy......

but somehow the dream faltered, became distant, flawed and i found myself overwhelmed by a crushing weariness - disconnecting me from the dream and awakening me to the harsh realization that our relationship, this romantic experiment was now over. so i exiled myself to a place of serenity far away from the clang and clamor of two hearts clashing. i withdrew from this union of you and i to escape the daily conflicts, the exhausting miseries and toxic tides. what was once invaluable as oxygen became a heavy burden multiplied in the now empty place where our dreams were once kindled.

these words are the final canto to our song which tell the sad tale of heart's promise betrayed and two tragic souls being laid to rest in the shadow of love's sepulcher.

end

Also by L. Ean Adams

DREAM Boudoir

A JOURNAL OF AMOROUS MUSINGS

www.ingramcontent.com/pod-product-compliance
Lightning Source LLC
Chambersburg PA
CBHW031458160726
47994CB00005B/2088